Jack and Z

Written by Jessica Ellis

Illustrated by Evelt Yanait

Collins

Jack is in bed.

Zain gets into bed too.

Jack turns the light off.

5

Zain thinks of hugs with Mum.

Zain thinks of his kitten.

He thinks of food. Yum!

Zain sees the moon.

He hears the rain.

Zain turns to Jack.

Zain feels better

 Review: After reading

Use your assessment from hearing the children read to choose any GPCs, words or tricky words that need additional practice.

Read 1: Decoding

- Ask the children to sound talk and blend each of the following words: f/ee/l/s, l/igh/t, m/oo/n, r/ai/n, h/ear/s.
- Can the children think of any words that rhyme with **light**? (e.g. *sight, fright, bright, fight, might, tight, height*)

Read 2: Prosody

- Model reading each page with expression to the children. After you have read each page, ask the children to have a go at reading with expression.
- Discuss how the characters are feeling. Show children how you use the characters' emotions to add expression to their voices for the speech bubbles.

Read 3: Comprehension

- Turn to pages 14 and 15 and ask the children to retell you the story using each picture as a prompt. Can the children remember how Zain was feeling at each part of the story? For every question ask the children how they know the answer. Ask:
  - Why do you think Jack turns the light off? (*because it is bedtime*)
  - On page 5, Zain is feeling sad. Why do you think he might be feeling sad? (*because he can't get to sleep/ because he is away from home/because he is frightened of the dark*)
  - What makes Zain feel better? (*thinking about good things; hugs with Mum, his kitten, food, the moon, the sound of the rain*)
  - Jack tells Zain to think of good things. What good things would you think of?
  - Would you like to have a sleepover? Explain why/why not.